INTRODUCTION

Following Ghosts is based on common sense, respect for the dog's natural abilities, positive reinforcement and keen observation skills. It is *not* a recipe book that will tell you how many tracks to lay every day for so many weeks in order to produce a TD, TDX or VST dog. It is an approach that allows thoughtful handlers to learn how to read, trust and assist their dog within the context of a tracking relationship.

Like much of dog training, standard approaches to tracking are full of unnecessary repetition, drilling and a lack of appreciation for what the dog is actually capable of. While we have great appreciation and respect for the countless handlers who struggled out of bed to lay tracks in the early morning dew, and drove countless miles to find the perfect tracking field, we hate to let the secret out: you didn't need to do all that to train a tracking dog. Really.

Imagine a tracking program that starts with tracks in your own backyard or neighborhood. Tracks that can be laid anytime, and just about anywhere. Sound impossible? It isn't. There is a catch, however. To be successful with this approach, you need a good relationship with your dog.

When talking to people interested in his approach to tracking, John has two very important questions: *Can you work with your dog off lead? Does your dog come when called?* The folks are often a little baffled by these questions; after all, a tracking dog works on lead all the time. What John is seeking is clues about the relationship between dog and handler.

Following Ghosts begins tracking by using the relationship with the owner as the motivation for putting that nose to the ground. When the handler moves out of sight, a dog who is motivated to find her will use all the skills he's got to solve the problem. While the dog initially begins by air scenting (the most efficient use of the nose), the first "track" has been set up in such a way that air scenting is not completely successful. Unable to find the handler by air scenting, the dog tries another skill he has - tracking. All on his own. And another tracking dog is born.

If the dog is uninterested in locating his handler, this approach won't work. While we sometimes up the ante by loading the handler with the dog's favorite toy, we do not resort to using food (for reasons discussed in detail later). Instead, we prefer to help the interested student work on improving their relationship. This is not always a popular solution with people who want to simply acquire a title, and see no reason for working on the relationship when a trail of hot dogs may convince the dog to track. To those people, we respectfully suggest that they try some of the other training methods. For us, the relationship between dog and handler stands as all important, and all training that we do aims hard at improving and maintaining a good relationship.

To become part of the tracking team, you have to be willing to read and trust your partner who, at the end of that long tracking line, is the only one who can see the ghosts that you're following. It is a relationship unlike any other shared by handlers and dogs. In learning to follow and trust your partner in pursuit of ghosts, you will find much more than a few articles. You'll find a whole new relationship with your dog.

REAL LIFE DEMANDS

When John began tracking over 14 years ago, his goal was the training of a multi-purpose search and rescue dog. Unhampered by any kennel club's official guidelines, he was guided only by the realities of what was needed from the dogs.

Fortunately ignorant of the "rules" regarding what a dog can and cannot do according to certain experts, he successfully trained three dogs to track, trail, and air scent (specific & non-specific scent). These dogs were used in search & rescue operations, and were also working police dogs called upon to do evidence searches, body part detection, cadaver searches (on land & in the water), building searches and drug detection work. Were these extraordinary dogs? Perhaps. Were these dogs able to use their natural gifts to a high degree thanks to a trainer who had no pre-conceived notions about the limits of their abilities? Definitely.

When you begin working with scent and your dog, the first thing to remember is that you are not teaching him anything new. You are simply defining how you want him to do what he naturally does - use his nose.

Regardless of the breed, each dog is born with his sense of smell operational. From his very first day, your dog has explored his world by using his nose. He knows all about scents floating through the air, scents pooled up on the ground, actual tracks left by both humans and animals, and can discriminate among the scents in his world to an astonishing degree. In this realm in which he has operated from birth, we are mere outsiders who, arrogantly at times, presume to "teach" the dog. This is as silly as a blind person trying to teach a sighted person how to see.

Many methods exist that rely heavily on the use of food to "teach" a dog about tracking and scent discrimination. As instructors, we have always wondered why these methods existed or why trainers felt them necessary. John was convinced that he was the subject of a practical joke when students in his Scent Workshop at Camp Dances With Dogs began earnestly explaining the cheese method and tie down approach to the scent discrimination exercise. When informed that he was hearing the truth, his only questions was "WHY?" A good question indeed.

Long before variable surface tracking became a popular buzzword, John and his Goldens (like countless search & rescue teams) demonstrated the amazing ability of a dog to work in heavily contaminated areas, such as an ongoing festival in a downtown urban setting when running a demonstration track through a crowd. This was not a crowd pleasing trick - it was a matter of necessity for effective search & rescue or police work.

The real world is a "variable surface." Rather than viewing the VST as the ultimate in tracking, we consider it the *natural starting point* when training a tracking dog.

Consider the "track" presented for the typical tracking search dog. It is midnight and raining when the search call comes in. At the search scene, at least 20 people are combing the woods, and have been doing so for several hours before someone decided to call for a dog team.

The scent object is either non-existent, has been contaminated through inappropriate handling or may consist of nothing more than a car door handle or the driver's seat. The "start" of your track may be a quarter-mile stretch where they "think" the lost person may have been seen. No one knows which direction the person went in, or even how long he's been gone.

Do search dogs find people under such conditions? You bet they do! Are they in search of hot dogs or cheese bits? Absolutely not.

Under such circumstances, dogs trained by John have successfully tracked bank robbers to a train station where, despite contrary reports from eyewitnesses that indicated the suspects had gone in the opposite direction, the station master confirmed that two men matching the robbers' description had indeed boarded an east bound train. His dogs have tracked a burglary suspect from the scene of a crime back to the suspect's own house - a track nearly 30 hours old and almost 3/4 mile long through suburbia.

How then is it that the obedience and tracking world has managed to not only underestimate the power of the dog's nose, but to make all exercises related to scent work such a complicated and frustrating issue for many dogs and handlers?

Combining our 36 years of experience of working with dogs, John and I decided to take a serious look at what was being taught as contrasted with what dogs have taught us is possible and amazingly easy. All of *Following Ghosts* is the result of observing dogs - and thinking about what they've taught us, not vice versa.

UNDERSTANDING SCENT

Consider scent in all its complexities as a ghost you cannot see nor ever understand, although your dog "sees" it quite clearly and understands it beyond our comprehension. We like to think of it like this: You are trying to understand someone who comes from a vastly different culture, who speaks a different language, and who is able to see ghosts you cannot.

A great deal of trust is involved here, as well as a willingness to believe that what your "interpreter" tells you about ghosts is accurate. This requires that you understand his language sufficiently to accurately hear what is being told to you, and that you can communicate your requests for information clearly.

Almost 1/8th of the dog's brain and over 50% of the internal nose is committed to olfaction.
W. Syrotuck
Scent & the Scenting Dog

For the dog, the sense of smell is not only powerful, but his **preferred** means of interpreting his world. Humans, on the other hand, are primarily visual. Whereas we might "look" at a new environment, the dog prefers to "smell" his world. We might remember how someone looks long before we recognize their scent, but for the dog it is reversed.

When you arrive at a show site or new training facility, you get out of your car and look around. You enter the building, and look around at the facility, the people in the room, etc. What does your dog do when you let him out of the car? Chances are very good that, given the opportunity, he drops his head and began exploring this new place with his nose.

We have observed that dogs often sit and look only after their noses have been allowed to explore, or if they've not been permitted to sniff. (These poor dogs often are found sitting with a slightly raised nose as they try to air scent all possible information available to them.)

To understand what you will be asking the dog when working in the realm of scent, try this exercise. Look at Figure 1 on the next page. The many shapes represents the complexities of odors available to the dog in just a *few square inches* of ground.

No matter how many times you were commanded to LOOK, could you begin to understand what shape which you were to "track?" You might guess, but the truth is no one shape has any more importance than another to you.

Figure 1

Is this because no one has taught you how to LOOK? If you're reading this, you've obviously possess considerable visual skills. Even though you can see them all quite clearly, we haven't helped you understand specifically how we want you to LOOK or what exactly you're looking for.

But I'm trying to teach you to LOOK. Like a good trainer trying to be helpful, I've added some clues in Fig. 2 to help you differentiate one shape from another. What happens now when you LOOK?

If you're like many people, your response is probably much like a dog's. You notice the dollar signs, just as a dog notices food scents, because money or even the symbol for money carries significance. But you still don't know what you're looking for.

10

Figure 2

It could be confusing if I allow you to focus on the dollar signs in Figure 2 hoping you would catch on that dollar signs *sometimes* are paired with what I really want you to track. Equally so, food can confuse dogs. What I have in mind has nothing to do with dollars, so I would not confuse you by using them as guides.

But what if I tell you to LOOK *only* at objects that contain the correct "scent" - that is, ones with the letter K? Go back and look again at Figure 2. Can you now follow the "track"? While you're looking again, notice how hard you have to concentrate to sort out not only the K's, but to follow the flow. (Hint: the "track" starts in the upper left hand corner.)

Once you clearly understood that K was the focus, it would not matter much what else was or was not paired with K. By making the other symbols larger or crowding the field with millions of letters or putting the letters on a wildly striped background, it could become much more difficult for you to sort the K's, but with sufficient motivation, concentration and practice, you could learn to LOOK with great skill.

Equally so, the dog who understands that human scent is the focus can learn to disregard other accompanying clues (crushed vegetation, food odors, etc.) that may at times also be present alongside human scent. Tracking requires intense focus and concentration from the dog to sort out the multitude of information offered to his nose. Why, then, would you choose a training method that possibly added to his confusion?

If the dog mistakenly believes that he is tracking food scent or crushed vegetation, he is easily lost when these coincidental "clues," which are completely irrelevant and unreliable, disappear, leaving only the human scent.

It is not much of a mystery why so many TD dogs find a TDX track so difficult. The TD track is laid on terrain without any remarkable change of cover - in other words, the vegetative cover should be relatively consistent throughout the track. The TDX tracks specifically calls for changes of cover (including plowed fields) as well as possible inclusion of "lightly traveled roads." What happens to the dog who does not understand that human scent and that alone is the desired focus? The "clues" he may have come to depend upon are missing.

While methods that focus on food and/or heavily disturbed vegetation obviously can and do work, the point is that they are unnecessary, even crude, considering the dog's innate skills in this department. More distressing is that these methods often set up dogs (and handlers!) for failure, ignoring the cardinal rule of dog training: *To learn, the dog must succeed.*

The key to our entire approach is this principle: *A dog knows how to use his nose - he only needs to learn HOW you want him to use it.*

You may find yourself muttering, "But that makes so much sense!" Because it does. As John will tell you, what he knows about tracking he learned from dogs. Because no one else knows as much about tracking and scent work as they do. The trick lies in understanding what they have to say.

HANDLER SKILLS

While the dog needs to master certain skills, so does the handler. Tracking is not a matter of hanging on to a lead and taking a stroll - it's teamwork. Independent of the dog's work, the handler should develop the following skills:

Trust Your Dog

This is the most obvious rule for tracking handlers, but often the hardest to actually apply. In a real tracking situation, you must be able to trust your dog since you will have few clues about the track's location. Your dog is interpreting a world beyond your comprehension. Second guessing the dog is not only unfair, but a sure fire way to confuse your dog. In order to trust your dog, you must learn to read your dog.

Reading Your Dog

If you cannot accurately interpret what your dog is telling you about the world of scent you have asked him to work in, then you will find it impossible to trust your dog. Each dog has a particular style of working - often, the signals that say "I'm on it" are subtle. It may be nothing more than a tip of the tail, or an attitude of the head. It may be a rhythm or a posture, or a combination of clues.

It is impossible to offer guidance or clarify what you want from the dog if you are unable to read him. And of course, you cannot accurately read your dog or offer any help to the dog if you don't know where the track is.

How will you tell at a tracking test whether Fido is still hot on the trail or merely taking a pleasant stroll unless you have learned to positively identify his every action?

Milo Pearsall
Scent - Training to Track, Search & Rescue

Know Where the Track is

Handlers often ask, "How do I get my dog to track accurately?" The answer is that dogs will be as accurate on the track as the handler allows them to be. If a handler is unsure where the track is, how can he make it clear to the dog that working on the scent that has drifted 2 feet from the actual track is not what is wanted? Many dogs do not actually track - they trail, working off of blown scent rather than the actual footsteps.

15

This is not due to sloppiness on the dog's part, but reflects the dog's very wise and effective use of his nose - on a track that is relatively fresh and/or under certain conditions, trailing *is* a very efficient approach. However, in our infinite human wisdom, we have decided that the dog should ignore what his experience tells him, and insist that he track when and as we ask him to. If that is what we want from the dog, then we need to realize that inaccurate tracking is not the dog's fault (simply a change in his use of his nose) but it is the fault of the *handler's* sloppiness.

Accurate tracking is no different from accurate obedience work. The more precision you insist on, the more precision you will get (up to the dog's physical limitations). Some dogs are capable of greater precision and/or more willing to bend to the artificial styles required in some tracking circles. Such stylized precision tracking may have little or nothing to do with how the dog actually works with scent. If it did, search dog handlers, working to save lives, would be employing that style of tracking instead of the more natural style that is prevalent in SAR work.

When beginning with any dog, knowing exactly where the track is allows you to read the dog's body language, show the dog what you want from him, and develop a working relationship that ultimately allows you to trust the dog.

Laying Tracks

Unfortunately, track laying is often one of the weakest of handler skills. Becoming proficient in track laying enables you to be helpful to your dog, and to any other handler/dog teams you may work with. If you don't know where the track is, how can you determine whether or not the dog is tracking accurately? While important for all handlers, strong track laying skills are critical for those who wish their dogs to track precisely, with a deep nose, as is often the case in Schutzhund tracking where points are deducted for imprecise style.

One of the easiest exercises a handler can practice is to simply lay a track, plotting it appropriately on paper and dropping one or more pennies along the way (in your track - not tossed to the side!). Mark your start, but not turns or the end. Wait for 15 minutes or even longer, then attempt to go back and, using your map, literally walk your track. If you're on target, you'll find your pennies. If not, try again! And again, and again, and again. . .

If you are fortunate to have a friend to work with, lay a track dropping pennies as in the individual exercise. Carefully map your track on paper. Give your friend your track map, and take his. Using his map as a guide, walk it. If his map is good, you'll find your "penny" articles. If not,

17

review the track with him walking beside you. The person who laid the track must know where that track is, or he cannot help you or your dog.

Great track layers can go back and find a track they've laid even days later. But practice, and a lot of it, is required. If you're like most people, remember to be creative - you can lay a track in the parking lot at work, or at the supermarket, or while walking to lunch. After all, a track is nothing more than where you've been, so anywhere you go, lay track!

Soft Hands

We teach a specific hand position for working the tracking lead that allows the handler to remain soft, attentive and responsive to the dog. While it may seem a little detail, exactly how you hold your lead affects your ability to breathe, walk and think.

Try this simple test: First, take several deep breaths and notice how your ribs, chest and abdomen move as you breathe in and out. Check your jaw - it should be relaxed. Next, bring your hands together towards the center of your body in typical track handling position, with one fist above the other, thumbs up and palms held near your diaphragm or even your chest. If you are like most folks, you'll have a habit of holding on with a fairly strong grip, so grab your imaginary lead as you usually do. Now, check your breathing. What breathing? Interfering with your breathing patterns interferes with your ability to think and move with clarity.

Our hand position is deliberately soft and open to help the handler continue to breathe, think and respond to the dog, and allows for more subtle information to flow up and down the lead.

For our soft hand position, first drop your hands towards your navel. Turn the palms up, with your thumbs pointing outwards and slightly down - imagine that you are softly supporting a thick rope that is coming out from your navel. Instead of a fist, hold your hands as if lightly containing a beautiful butterfly who will be crushed if you tighten your grip. Allow the lead to lay across both palms, passing between thumbs and forefingers. Use your thumbs to control the lead and the dog, slowing with a little pressure or bringing the dog to a complete halt with full pressure and a slight upwards cocking of the wrist.

To test the difference that this hand position makes to your ability to both read and communicate with the dog, put a friend at the end of your tracking lead. First, without telling them which hand position you're using, experiment with your old position and the new soft hands. In both positions, try gently slowing your "dog" as well as stopping her completely. Go back and forth between the two positions, noticing the changes in your body, breathing and tension levels. Ask your "dog" for some feedback - "How does this feel?"

Next, close your eyes and have your "dog" move as if on a track. Your "dog" can hesitate, pull hard, take turns, circle, etc. Using both hand positions, see what information you can read coming up the lead. One of John's students was shocked to open her eyes and realize that in the soft hand position, she was able to clearly read his direction changes - which were only 2-4" either way! In the old hand position, he had to move more than a foot before she could clearly feel that change.

For those handlers whose dogs pull hard, it is paradoxical that one way to slow the dog down is to relinquish the "death grip" which only encourages and enables the dog to pull harder. In order to pull, the dog must have something to pull against. Strangely, when freed from the restraint of a hard grip, dogs often slow down. Avoid clutching the line - even on a strong dog, you can use soft hands. This keeps you relaxed, and able to read the signals coming up the line to you.

SKILL BUILDING IN THE DOG

Ideally, just as a child learns the whole alphabet
before beginning to read words, and words before
sentences and sentences before *War & Peace* becomes a
class assignment, the tracking dog is introduced to and
allowed to master each necessary skill very early on in his
training. Sometimes these skills are worked on
individually, and more often, in varying combinations and
proportions with other skills.

Once these skills have been established, it is then easy to
build the dog's ability to concentrate for longer periods and
greater distances. The tracking dog's skill list reads
something like this:

- ✓ Identify scent to be followed
- ✓ Locate starting point
- ✓ Determine direction of track
- ✓ Follow track - through turns, over
changes of surface and regardless of
cross tracks
- ✓ Locate articles

IDENTIFYING SCENT TO BE FOLLOWED

In our opinion, many of the methods currently used to train tracking unnecessarily confuse the dog. This begins with the scent that the dog believes you are asking him to follow. Our goal is a dog who understands from the beginning that human scent, and only human scent, is the scent of choice. Experience will teach the dog that this human scent may be paired with crushed vegetation, or asphalt, or sand or gravel or any surface you can think of, but these additional scents are **coincidental**, not the objective.

By beginning tracking with runaways, we encourage the dog to actively use *human scent* to locate his handler. Initially, this is air scenting and trailing since the handler is working **across the wind**, leaving a considerable swath of blown scent for the dog to follow. This is easy for any dog to follow, and quickly builds enthusiasm and confidence.

It is the next step that lays the foundation for the dog following human scent, regardless of any other scents that may accompany it. After running an appropriate distance **across the wind**, the handler turns **with the wind** and walks slowly or crawls a short distance before hiding or laying down out of sight. Handlers who cannot crawl or crouch should switch to slow, closely spaced steps before hiding or laying down out of sight.

The dog eagerly starts off, following the air scent to the place where he believes the handler to be (often visually marking the spot), but to his surprise, when he arrives, the handler is no where to be seen. Air scenting now is no longer effective - the dog is upwind of the scent pool. The natural response of the dog is to drop his head to the only scent available to him - your track. At this point (and not before!) the command to *track* is given, along with praise.

Occasionally, dogs need encouragement to drop their head. This may reflect a physical problem, or simply a lack of experience using the nose. To encourage a head drop, the handler should place an article at the point where he has changed direction to go into the wind. The handler need do nothing more than carry it that short distance and simply place it as they make the turn.

As the dogs search around, they usually spot the object visually and immediately drop their heads to check it out. From that point, most dogs then discover the track without any help. If necessary, the person working the lead can encourage the dog to further investigate that area by gesturing quietly toward the article. (Very, very rarely, John will use a small piece of food on that article to help motivate dogs who don't care much where the heck their handler has gone off to! But this is a "band-aid" - that relationship needs more help than a hot dog slice.)

This approach is surprisingly simple, but takes full advantage of the dog's natural tendency to switch between all three scenting styles of air scenting, trailing and tracking. If you take the time to observe a dog who is working off lead, on his own time, you'll see him utilizing all three styles.* When air scenting (a highly effective means of working scent) fails, the dog switches to trailing blown scent, and that failing, as it does in our setup, the dog must drop his head and resort to tracking.

A distinct preference for a certain style of working scent can be seen among individual dogs as young as six weeks old. While almost any dog can be trained to track, some dogs seem to find it "natural."

24

Locate The Starting Point

Long before you worry about the dog being able to locate the start of a track, you should consider the following ways in which the handler can make it difficult and/or unpleasant for the dog to even begin.

Stomp, stomp, shuffle, shuffle - while these are great dance steps, but they are not necessary for laying a scent pad to begin a track. We have seen young or very inexperienced dogs just beginning search & rescue training accurately mark spots along the trail where the "victim" stopped just long enough to check wind direction with a quick puff of wind powder or a flick of a lighter. There was no scuffing or stomping, simply a person standing normally for perhaps 10-15 seconds before continuing on. This pause allows for an easily detectable amount of scent to pool in the subtle depressions left by the footprints.

The average human sheds roughly 40,000 skin cells - every minute!

Wherever you feel the need to leave a strong scent, such as on a start, avoid disturbing vegetation (thus confusing the dog with this strong background scent). Instead, stand

25

quietly for anywhere from a few seconds to a minute.
Want to leave a really great starting pad? Try sitting on the
spot for a few minutes, or kneeling on all fours - both
techniques take advantage of the natural skin cell shedding
and allow a scent pool to build at the spot without adding
highly disturbed vegetation to the mix. *Use these
techniques with care - unless the track is well aged, such
intensity of scent can confuse, not assist, the dog.*

Several common training techniques regarding the start can
contribute to the dog's confusion. One is creating a very
heavy scent pad (usually by shuffling or scuffing) in an
effort to make it "clear" for the dog. Depending on the age
of the scent, wind speed/direction, such a heavy scent pad
can diffuse over a very large area, making it more difficult
for the dog to pinpoint the track itself (especially if the dog
has been allowed to work on blown scent and not held to
the track itself).

A heavy scent pad can also "flood" the dog's nose, a
problem compounded when handlers insist on downing the
dog at the start. Chances are good that the dog can detect a
strong scent pad from a normal standing position or even
several feet away, with no need to get his nose right on the
ground. John has seen many dogs track the track layer **to**
the starting flag!

Handlers who can read their dogs know when the dog has sorted the scent and is ready to begin - this may be nothing more than a quick sniff or two. Repeated insistence on showing the dog the scent can irritate the dog. You must know how your dog indicates that he's ready to work.

Downing at the start can also depress the dog, or inadvertently (depending on your training methods for obedience work) give the dog the impression that he is being punished. Softer dogs who are highly sensitive to the handler may view the down as a rebuke. This is especially true when the handler uses a loud/firm command, uses any form of physical "correction" for the down, and/or is tense or nervous.

> Corrections serve no purpose and must be avoided: no handler can possibly tell what the dog does or does not smell.
> *Milo Pearsall*
> **Scent - Training To Track, Search & Rescue**

Tougher dogs may be unwilling to assume a down when they are gearing up for working a track. Insistence here may create resistance, and cost the handler in cooperation and respect from the dog, and even escalate into a confrontational situation. If the handler's misinformed attitude is one of "I can't let him get away with that!" the handler may resolve the problem *they created* by using force in the form of a leash, collar or verbal correction.

Avoid using any method for starting a track which involves corrections, subordinate body postures from the dog, dominant posture/behavior from the handler, and which unnecessarily floods the dog's nose with scent. A happy, upbeat start based on accurate reading of the dog's response to the scent should be your aim.

Consider having a start flag as a luxury which allows you to define a relatively narrow area where the track begins. In search and rescue tracking, a handler is often given a scent article along with vague instructions such as "the track begins on the eastern boundary of this 25 acre field." The dog must then work to find the start before even beginning the track. As with any training, think about educating your dog well beyond the narrow requirements of an AKC, CKC or Schutzhund track.

As tracking progresses, John will often set two flags 100' apart - the track starts somewhere between those two points and the dog must find it. Obviously, knowing that your dog is capable of working in that fashion makes it much easier to trust him at the start.

Determining Direction of Track

Our good friend Katrene Johnson, an experienced search trainer, told us about the day she was sitting out in the woods while her search dog, Razzy, was exploring nearby. She watched a chipmunk dart out from cover, cross a fallen log and continue on to a woodpile. Chipmunks not only have very small feet, but also move very quickly. A few minutes later, Razzy wandered over and caught the chipmunk's scent on the log. With a half inch move of his nose to the left and then to the right, Razzy sorted the direction the chipmunk had headed and tracked it to the woodpile. Your own dog probably does similar directional sorts dozens of times each day in the backyard.

Imagine that you've been sent on a life or death mission to find a member of a road crew who is repainting the stripes on the road. Following the directions you've been given, you arrive at a T-intersection where you can see the freshly painted stripes. But glancing up and down the road, you can see no sign of the road crew - just freshly painted stripes in both directions. How could you determine which direction the road crew had been working in?

The answer would found by looking at the stripes for clues as to which were drier and thus had been laid earlier, and which stripes were more recently painted. Obviously, the road crew can be found by following the track in the direction of the increasingly "fresher" stripes. Paint drying is a fair, though rough, analogy to aging scent.

But what if that road crew had laid the stripes one direction, then come back and painted over them again in the other direction? Or even triple painted them by heading off again in the original direction?

In the same fashion, double or triple laying a track, while decidedly increasing the scent in that area, can also confuse a dog as to the direction of the track. Double or triple laying is traditionally done at the start and on turns - two areas where many dogs and handlers have problems.

We feel that some of the problems can be attributed to confusion of track direction. We prefer to prevent the problem through correct early training of the start and turns, and if required to trouble shoot a trained dog, might recommend a slower pace and/or more closely spaced steps instead of double or triple laying a track.

Interestingly, all of the studies that we have read that attempted to prove or disprove the dog's ability to detect track direction came to the same conclusion: dogs can't do much better than chance in detecting track direction. Unfortunately, each of these studies had one serious flaw - every dog had been trained using popular methods that included double and triple laying as well as food.

Since search dogs, which are not trained in that fashion, seem to be quite good at determining track direction (indeed, they have to be or they're not much use in a search situation), we feel that the problem most likely lies not with the dogs' abilities, but with the training methods used long before the test began.

There is always a reason for a dog's apparent difficulty on track.

Glen Johnson
Tracking Dog

Following the Track

Good tracking requires focused attention from the dog, which can be very tiring mentally and physically. The dog's ability to concentrate should be built slowly, never pushing him past the point where such concentration ceases to be enjoyable. To be effective while following a track, the dog must develop skills in handling turns, changes of surface/cover and cross tracks.

Turns

If you've ever watched your dog follow the meandering path of a cat, rabbit or mouse, you know that the concept of straight line tracks has little to do with the real world our dogs inhabit but are merely concessions to the human half of the team. Without straight line track legs, how many of us could truly say where we had been?

Your dog doesn't need straight lines, and all of his natural experiences with his nose have included turns, switchbacks, back tracks and cross tracks. Many methods recommend "building the dog up to turns" by running increasingly long, straight tracks until the dog can track X number of yards before turns are introduced. We're not sure why this is so, and find this actually detrimental to the development of good tracking skills.

We prefer to introduce turns and changes of surface before increasing distance. To understand why, consider your own experiences with these situations:

> A. You are driving down the interstate.
> While not a familiar road, you know you
> will be driving for many miles - your exit is
> #74 and you began just past exit #50.

How much attention do you pay to the road? Do you carefully observe the lines painted on the road, watching them go by? Do you anxiously check every road sign as soon as it becomes visible, or do you only glance at them casually to confirm where you are?

> B. You are driving down a country road.
> An unfamiliar road, it twists and turns. The
> lanes are not clearly marked, and lane
> widths keep changing from wide to very
> narrow. At times, the road is paved, and at
> other times it deteriorates into mud and
> gravel. It is hard to tell if you are on the
> road or driving across someone's farmland.
> There are no marked exits, and landmarks
> you need may be partially hidden.

How much attention do you pay to the road? How important do lane markings become? Do you carefully check all road signs and landmarks?

On long, straight tracks, dogs react very much like a relaxed driver on the interstate - they plug into the direction of travel and do not need to do much more than "check" that they're on the right path. Tracking judge Ted Hoesel has carefully watched video of such dogs - he discovered that the dogs did not *constantly* track but only took a confirming sniff an average of *every four strides.*

Instead of building the dog's ability to concentrate, we feel long, straight tracks can contribute to careless tracking and to boredom. After all, for pure interest while driving, who takes the interstate? As long as the dog is not overwhelmed with complexity beyond his abilities, few things build focus in a tracking dog like a truly challenging track. And challenging does not necessarily equal long.

Early training which focuses on long, straight tracks can also lead some dogs into a form of pattern training that we call "appearance tracking" - that is, they give all the appearances of tracking (nose down, moving ahead with enthusiasm). In reality, they are simply offering a posture and behavior that they have learned makes their handler happy without really understanding what they were supposed to be doing.

John has watched many dogs at tracking trials who, taking
unintentional cues from their handlers, would happily
strike out in any given direction, moving in a straight line,
and giving the appearance of tracking while in fact, the
track ran in the opposite direction! (How handlers
inadvertently train this response in their dogs will be
discussed later.)

By introducing turns and surface changes *early*, you
encourage interest and help the dog build the skills he will
need. Practically speaking, this approach also allows you
to train almost anywhere - even a short 10 yard track could
have several turns and changes of surface! Once the dog
has mastered the basic skills, it is a simple matter to
gradually increase the distance as the dog's ability to
concentrate for greater periods increases. Not incidentally,
early skill development leads to repeated success which
builds confidence, leading to the dog's willingness to
concentrate for longer periods.

Changes of Surface

Failure to introduce a variety of surfaces in early training
can also contribute to confusion as to what is the scent to
be followed. Dogs worked only in relatively consistent
ground cover may fail to realize that it is *human scent*, and
not crushed vegetation/ground disturbance, that is to be

tracked. This is often a large factor in the failure of many TD dogs on TDX tracks where regulations call specifically for change of cover. Of course, the new VST title highlights the difficulties of varied surfaces, especially for dogs who may not have had exposure to multiple surfaces.

A dog introduced to gravel, sand, clay, various vegetation and surfaces early on understands easily that the only common thread is human scent - all other scents are purely coincidental. Early surface changes also encourage greater focus, as different surfaces hold varying degrees of scent. Variable surface tracking presents no problem for a dog started using our approach.

Dogs must learn to distinguish between the "background" scents and the scent to be followed. To accomplish this, trainers need to expose to the dog to human scent in as many contexts as possible.

John worked with a group of Texas police handlers whose dogs found it nearly impossible to track across a lush, grassy field, yet easily tracked across a gravel parking lot. Since their native environment was typically devoid of lush vegetation, the dogs had never before encountered human scent in that context, and the very strong presence of vegetative disturbances made it very hard going for them.

Conversely, a Midwest group's dogs could easily work on the grass but were totally lost on surfaces without vegetation. It is not that the scent was not present for either group of dogs, just that they had not been trained to handle these scenting situations.

> . . . Dogs, like humans, may become very
> disturbed by very strong unfamiliar smells.
> In this case, exposure to a wide variety of
> odors and environments should be a part
> of the dog's training.
>
> *W. Syrotuck*
> **Scent & The Scenting Dog**

Cross Tracks

As a Ranger, John lived within a 1400 acre forest preserve where AKC tracking tests were often held in the fields behind his house. He always found it amusing when trackers talked about the tracking fields being "uncontaminated" for the day of the test. Here's the "traffic" he noted in just the evening before and the morning of the test: Countless deer, rabbits, birds & assorted insects and small mammals, a group of coyotes, a troop of Boy Scouts, at least a dozen horses and riders, hikers with and without dogs, forest preserve personnel checking on plantings in the field, and bicyclists illegally off trail. That's just what he personally witnessed!

It is not only unrealistic but unnecessary to worry about cross tracks and contamination. **There are no uncontaminated tracking areas**, except perhaps on the moon. More important, the dog's astounding olfactory capabilities allows him to distinguish in incredibly fine increments the age of any particular track or scent.

Working with a scent discrimination pile and an overly enthusiastic retriever, John was able to show the handler how the dog retrieved all of the articles back to her in a very precise way - from the article most recently scented backwards to the very first article put out in the pile. For some of these articles, the time difference was no more than 30 seconds, and some had been deposited in the pile with tongs!

It is not uncommon in John's tracking lessons for the track to occur in areas where he and/or the handler has already walked - sometimes repeatedly. While he doesn't go out of his way to point this out to handlers, they occasionally catch on when they ask, "When do we start training for cross tracks?" He then has them review where they've been during the lesson and where the tracks have been.

To their amazement, they realize that not only has their novice dog been working with cross tracks all along, but that they've been sorting out cross tracks from their own handler and the track layer! Cross track training should occur naturally, and deliberately laid cross tracks should not present a problem.

One final note on cross tracks. I once spent some time with a tracking handler who explained at length the problem she had with her dog. It seems that he refused to acknowledge cross tracks and simply plowed on with the (correct) track he had been working. She found this very upsetting, and spent several months working with him so that he would stop at cross tracks, check carefully in all directions and then resume tracking. In her own words, " How can I trust him if he doesn't tell me that he's really checked the cross tracks?"

I wasn't sure whether I found it amusing or sad that when questioned, this handler admitted that the dog had never, ever gone off track to follow a cross track. For a good tracking dog, cross tracks may be not acknowledged in any way, just as a driver does not need to read signs for exits that he instantly recognizes are not the one he wants.

Have sense.

Locate Articles

Years of experience with "real life" tracking and police work evidence searches taught John that his dogs needed to be able to locate articles ranging from a gum wrapper to a discarded soda can. While different materials definitely hold scent differently, the wise tracking trainer teaches the dog to respond to as many types of articles as possible. This is necessary for a VST track, and also is extremely useful in every day life when your dog can help you find the keys or earrings you dropped.

Depending upon the material that the article is made of, your dog's indications may change. Hard plastic or metal articles will obviously hold less scent than cloth, leather or some softer plastics. Work with a variety of objects and pay close attention to your dog's body language. On an object that saturates easily, the dog may give one type of alert and possibly from a much greater distance than on an object which holds less scent. Know the difference.

Whatever your preferred means of having the dog indicate an article, you need to treat article indication as a separate exercise to be taught outside of the actual tracking situation. Some people expect the dog to retrieve the article to them. And while an article retrieve may work well for a natural retriever, not all dogs are as willing to retrieve any old object.

Others look for the dog to sit or down at the article, and wait for the handler to pick it up before going on. While these are fine, watch your dog carefully to be sure that he finds these positions agreeable. No matter how pleased you may appear with the find, following it up with a compulsive reinforcement of the "down" command will not make for a happy tracking dog.

As with the start, be aware that your choice of article indication and your method for teaching it can inadvertently create an unpleasant situation or negative associations with the article

Whatever indication you choose, the basic rule is a simple one - the dog must always be praised for finding an article, and your timing such that the dog understands that the praise is for finding, not sitting or laying down. One can never be too generous with praise of a dog who has made a find.

At one seminar, a woman presented a German Shepherd with some tracking experience. She complained that the dog lacked enthusiasm, and often failed to indicate articles to her satisfaction. John laid a track with several articles, and then walked along to observe what was happening.

While the dog tracked acceptably, there was a noticeable change in the dog when she detected the article. With a tentative wag of her tail, she stopped and looked back at the handler with a question in her eyes. The handler's response? "DOWN!" The dog dropped, ears laid back and obviously believing that the handler was unhappy with her. THEN the handler reached for the article as she said, "Good dog!"

It doesn't take a genius to figure out that from the dog's point of view, finding the articles was not a very pleasant situation. Instead of an ecstatic praise response from the handler, the dog received a somewhat harsh command, and for compliance with that command, received some moderate praise. At no time did the dog receive praise (as the dog perceived it) for finding the article.

Finding an article should be an exceptionally pleasant experience for the dog. Don't be afraid to really get excited and heap praise on your dog's head. And by all means, avoid setting the dog up for any unpleasantness in association with the articles.

It may be helpful to you to think of the entire track as a series of smaller tracks, each leading to an article. From the dog's point of view, any track is a series of tracks which *arbitrarily* ends when you, the handler, determine that you have found the "last" article. Sound odd?

Remember that to the dog, it is very clear that the track layer was not airlifted from the site of the last article - a track continues on from there, just as it has from all previous articles. Nothing changes to let the dog know that he has "finished" the track - it goes on and he knows it!

This is very different from the search & rescue dog whose track ends, hopefully, with the find of the person who laid the track. (Few dogs look as dismayed or unfulfilled as a search dog called off a track for whatever reason.) That track does have an end that the dog understands - traditional tracking offers the dog no such clear end point. And as in all dog training adventures, an end point or exercise goal that is known only to the handler and appears nonsensical or unfathomable from the dog's point of view is always a problematic area rife with potential misunderstandings.

At each article, as you praise your dog, do so with the joy you might reserve only for the final article. Keep in mind that only you know the final article is the "end" - your dog does not. The dog has successfully completed the track from your previous point (the start or another article) - praise him! This will help you as a handler avoid the dreaded "last article syndrome."

This syndrome occurs most often at tracking tests, where handlers become increasingly more uptight as the track goes on. Without realizing it, they can translate this tension to their dog. Some dogs may come to associate the last article with the really strange and unpleasant behavior of the handler, and thus begin to slow down and lose confidence towards the final legs of the track. John has seen one dog actively avoid the final article when that became the place where the handler dumped all of her displeasure with the dog's performance over the entire track.

For fun, and to increase the dog's excitement, try laying tracks which have real end points and a great "article" - a live person waiting to join you in praising and playing with the dog. This serves to increase the dog's motivation, and to highlight the "end" as a real, understandable point. Of course, if you are asking the dog retrieve any article he finds, you might want to skip having the dog retrieve that "final article. . ."

GUIDELINES FOR
A TRACKING PROGRAM

Following Ghosts is not a recipe - it's an approach, a mind set, even a philosophy. These are our guidelines for developing a tracking program that works for you and your dog.

Due to the unique interaction of every dog/handler team, any good tracking instructor will alter the lessons for maximum benefit. We agree strongly with Glen Johnson's philosophy that *every track must have a specific objective.* That is, with every track, you are trying to develop a particular skill, or accomplish a certain goal. Correctly done, each track builds on previous tracks, enlarging both the dog and handler's understanding and proficiency.

While it is entirely possible for a dog to work in very hot conditions, we do not recommend it. This is not due to the difficulties of scent work under those conditions (though the dog's nose must be kept wet and water offered frequently) but instead is a reflection of our concern for the dog's safety. Search & rescue dogs must be worked even under extreme conditions to prepare them for such work,

45

simply because they may well be asked to do so on a life or death basis.

However, for tracking tests and any "sport," we feel that weather that you and/or your dog finds uncomfortable quickly takes the fun out of the game rather quickly, and can lead to serious conditions such as heatstroke - at either end of the lead.

Be fair - a sport is only a sport when it is enjoyable for ALL participants. This does not, however, excuse you from tracking in the rain (unless your dog hates rain and you're willing to give up your spot in the Tracking Test when it rains and rains and rains!)

Basic Guidelines

> ✳ **Encourage nose-down tracking early on with correct use of wind direction**

> ✳ **Early tracks short, highly motivational - dog is always successful**

> ✳ **Introduce varied surfaces early**
> *Even very short straight track may include several changes of surface. Be creative!*

46

✻ **Introduce turns as soon as dog reliably tracks nose-down.** *Clearly mark turns well by slow and/or closely spaced steps just before & through the turn before taking your normal stride again. You may also use "soft" turns - turns which have greater than a 90 degree angle to them. Gradually increase the angle of the turn until the dog has mastered true right angle turns.*

✻ **Increase complexity of track (multiple surfaces & turns) while keeping track short.** *This keeps the dog focused without boring him or tiring him as he builds skill.*

✻ **Emphasize the dog's need to actively work for turns by using your normal striding through turns, altering the angle of the turn, and "jumping off" turns.** *Once the dog has mastered all sorts of turns - soft (greater than 90 degrees - ideal for beginners), sharp (approaching right angles - moderate skill level) and even acute (less than 90 degrees - more advanced), you can progress to "jump-off" turns.*

For a "jump-off" turn, simply stop, then leap 2-3 feet or so to where you want the track to continue. This gap in the track forces the dog to actively seek the new direction.

✳ **When dog can handle at least 4-8 turns and multiple surfaces on a short track (under 100 yards total), begin to age scent in 5-10 minute progressions up to 45 minutes aging.**

✳ **Once dog is proficient with 45 minute old track, jump to tracks at least 1 ½ hours old and progress to of 10-15 minute increases until the dog can run 2 ½ -3+ hour old tracks.** *This avoids the "trough" period which occurs between 45 minutes to 1 ½ hours of aging. The trough is an extremely difficult time period for the dog to work and should be avoided until greater skill is developed.*

✳ **When dog is working well at 2 ½ - 3 hours of aging, go back to working tracks between 45 minutes and 1 ½ hours old.** *This "trough" is the most difficult time window for a dog to work.*

✳ **Build proficiency in complexity of track and age of track before gradually increasing length of track.** *Lengthening the track is the easiest of all for the dog - IF he knows how to handle the variables of turns, surfaces and aging first.*

✳ **Throughout the training, keep articles varied and interesting.** *Thrift shops are great sources of inexpensive items easily tucked in a pocket. Use plastic, wood, metal, paper - anything! For pure amazement value, try dropping a coin or two - you may be surprised by your dog's response.*

✳ **NEVER scold a dog or fail to praise him** - *even if he locates an article you don't believe is part of his track. Every tracking instructor worth their name can tell you of countless inadvertent or unsuspecting drops by track layers (from bobby pins to gum wrappers to car keys!) Avoid calling your dog off something you don't believe to be an article - he may be right. Check it out, praise the dog and go on.*

✳ **Keep your hands soft.** *The tracking line is your primary means of communication - soft hands keep you breathing and open to what's going on at the dog's end of the lead.*

✳ **BREATHE!** *While this may seem obvious, your breathing affects the dog as well as yourself. Many handlers, while concentrating, forget to breathe in AND out!*

✳ **TRUST your dog** *When in doubt, follow the dog. Don't over analyze or try to out think your dog. He's the only one who knows what's really going on.*

✳ **PRAISE your dog** *Be sincere and generous with praise - even when the track didn't go well or mistakes were made. Always let him know he's a genius for finding anything, even the unexpected.*

✳ **Occasionally back up in training and give the dog some hot, easy tracks.**
There's nothing like a "piece of cake" track to build a dog's motivation and enthusiasm.

COMMON HANDLING ERRORS

More often than not, it is the handler, and not the dog, who is to blame for tracking problems. Here are some of the most common handling errors:

● **Not reading dog**

Learn how your dog tells you he's "got it," and know how to recognize the instant he's lost and in need of help. In addition to watching the dog while he's tracking, spend time watching your dog while on his own time, and observe how he uses his nose. A video camera can also be helpful - have someone tape your dog while he's tracking for replay and analysis at a later time. If the track layer can watch the video with you, they should be able to tell you to what and why the dog is responding along the way.

● **Not knowing where track is**

If you don't know where the track is, you can't learn to read your dog or help him. You may need to practice laying and then following tracks - without your dog. Anyone who lays a track for you should be able to accurately plot their path,

51

and be able to work with you and your dog to offer instant advice should a question arise.

● Pushing the dog

Dogs are highly sensitive to handler position, signals, even breathing and muscular tension. Pushing a dog can be as simple as stepping forward - dogs often interpret this as the handler saying "yes, the track goes this way." Remember, tracking is teamwork, and your dog is sometimes quite willing to take your advice, even if it's not good advice. There is a fine line between *knowing* where the track is and *showing* where the track is!

● Shaping appearance, not action

This inadvertent training comes from handlers who, unable to accurately read their dogs, eagerly reinforce what they believe to be tracking. This is not uncommon when handlers guide their dogs on the track rather than waiting for a strong commitment from the dog.

● Not waiting for commitment from dog

When you know how to read your dog, there is a clear signal of commitment when a dog is on the track. Handlers often rush their dogs, especially at starts and turns instead of waiting for the dog to truly commit. Be patient!

● Continuing on when dog is not on track

Whether the dog has shifted to trailing or is simply messing around, allowing the dog to continue when he is not actually on the track sends a very clear message to the dog. Unfortunately, the message is that careless, unfocused work is acceptable, perhaps even desirable. The moment you see your dog not working on the track to the degree of accuracy you want, you must STOP, moving forward only when the dog goes back to tracking.

● Stepping off the track

Handlers sometimes make the mistake of stepping off the track in the misguided notion that the dog is being given room to work out the problem. If you need to give the dog some room to cast about, step backwards precisely (as much as possible) in your own footsteps to a distance that leaves the dog some room to work on finding the track from the last point you *know* he had the track. Stay on the track at all times - if helpful, view the dog's nose as clearing a safe passageway for your feet, and only step in areas that have been "cleared" by the dog. Let the excess lead drag in a straight line behind you - this will serve as a visual clue of exactly where you've been should you need to back up.

● Inadvertent signaling

Dogs are extraordinarily good at reading subtle cues, including the manner in which you hold your tracking line, your hands, and your body. To keep the line from interfering with the dog, some handlers raise the line quite high when they halt to let the dog work out a turn.

Especially when the handler knows where the track is or is informed of the track's direction by a "helpful" coach, the handler may unknowingly relax, take a breath, drop the hand and/or change the tension on the lead as the dog works towards the correct direction, thus giving the dog an inadvertent signal. Dogs can and do become dependent upon this guidance.

John recalls watching one handler in a tracking test do exactly this. At the first turn, she held her line high while the dog circled looking for the track, then dropped her hand when the dog turned in what she believed was the correct direction. The dog plowed ahead in the direction the handler had inadvertently signaled, and looked like he was tracking beautifully. The only problem was that the track actually had turned in the opposite direction. The handler's comment? "This dog always has problems at turns..."

● Not enough water

For optimal function, a dog's nose needs to be kept moist. Smart handlers offer their dogs water before a track, and depending on the weather and ground conditions, carry water to refresh the dog's nose along the way. Handlers should also be aware that tracking is very tiring for a dog, and like any hard working dog, water is not only appreciated but necessary.

● Down on start

As already discussed, be careful when using a downed start, as this can depress the dog, irritate him, trigger a defensive response, or even escalate into a confrontation.

CONCLUSION

Tracking stands uniquely alone as the dog sport where a handler must learn to rely on and trust his dog. Even in herding, where the dog's greater instinctive skill in understanding and working sheep easily outstrips the handler's, the herding handler at least has the advantage of being able to *see* the sheep. Imagine trying to work a herd of sheep visible only to the dog! In essence, that is what the tracking handler faces - the "ghosts" of unseen and dimly understood forces shaping the dog's responses.

This booklet does not assume to cover all of the intricacies of tracking. We've left out a world of information on both dog and handler, and not even touched on the complexities of how scent, wind, weather and topography combine, and how it all comes together or falls apart. We have tried to present some new perspectives and provoke new ways of thinking about tracking.

In the next few years, we plan to expand *Following Ghosts* into a complete, detailed book. If you've enjoyed this booklet, and found the material helpful, or if you have comments or suggestions, we'd like to hear from you.

Happy Tracking!